Sanctuary

The Shamanic Art of Sacred Space:
Workbook 2

Gwilda Wiyaka, CSI

Berthoud, CO
www.FindYourPathHome.com
303-775-3431

© 2004, 2011, 2012 Gwilda Wiyaka
Path Home Media & Publishing
Berthoud, CO

www.FindYourPathHome.com
TouchIn@FindYourPathHome.com
303-775-3431

All rights reserved. This book may not be reproduced in whole or in part, without written permission from the publisher, except by a reviewer who may quote brief passages in a review; nor may any part of this book be reproduced, stored in a retrieval system, or transmitted in any form or by any means: electronic, mechanical, photocopying, recording, or other, without written permission from the publisher.

Cover design:	Gwilda Wiyaka Trixie Phelps
Cover photograph:	Shutterstock® Images
Illustrations:	Gwilda Wiyaka
Prepared for publication:	Trixie Phelps
Photographs:	Laura Curtsinger Heather Miller

Dedication

To my children, Laura & Jason Curtsinger and Mark and Heather Miller, for their unwavering love faith and support.

To all of my clients, students, and spiritual teachers without whom this workbook could not have been written.

Table of Contents

Forward xi

Chapter 1: What is Sacred Space? 1

Chapter 2: The Medicine Wheel 3

Chapter 3: The Four Directions 5

Chapter 4 Gratitude 9

Chapter 5: Drawing on Ancient Principles 11

Chapter 6: Why We Need Sacred Space 13

Chapter 7: Tools for Setting Sacred Space 15

Chapter 8: Steps for Setting Sacred Space 17

Chapter 9: Building an Altar 19

Chapter 10: Calling In Your Power 23

Chapter 11: Relating to the Elements 25

Chapter 12: Demystifying the Mysterious 27

Chapter 13: Stuff 29

Chapter 14: Sacred Space a State of Grace 31

Chapter 15: Sacred Space Journey Assignments 33

About Path Home Shamanic Arts School 37

Resources 39

CD's and MP3's available for this workbook 39

Sanctuary

As I hike in the high Colorado Mountains

The trail gently winds down to a stream then opens up

Entering an ancient stand of trees

Light filters through the pines casting rays of warmth

Onto the cool rich loam at their bases

The air, kissed by the moisture from the bubbling stream

Brushes past my face in a tender caress

As I settle down on a flat boulder to rest

Birds, silenced by my arrival take up their song

I calm my body, still my mind and I am there

Sanctuary

I step from the Arizonan sun

Through an adobe archway

Into the courtyard sheltered by trees

Water in a three tiered fountain

Cascades into the base filling the air with its vapor

The perfume from the flower bed

Dances on the gentle breeze

In the midst of flowering cactus, vines and roses

Her blue robes faded by the sun

Statuary of the Madonna

Stands timeless and serene

I step from the path and sit on a sandstone bench.

A small lizard, disturbed by my presence

Scampers under a leaf

Mourning doves call to each other

From the branches of the deciduous trees

I close my eyes, embrace the moment and I am there

Sanctuary

Leaving the busy city street

I pass under a torii gate, through the red door

Onto the polished hardwood floor

Of the small entry way

I remove my shoes and don the slippers

Thoughtfully left there for my use

My friend greets me

Inviting me into the sparsely furnished room

We sit on soft cushions next to a low table

Flanked by bamboo plants in tall black vases

A brass fountain with floating chimes

Sings softly

She pours tea into white porcelain cups

The sound of the liquid joining the symphony

Of running water and chimes

I lift the handless cup to my face

And inhale its jasmine essence

Time stands still

I close my eyes in pleasure and I am there

Sanctuary

I never cease to wonder

At this mystic place found many places

This hallowed ground

Nestled magically amongst the mundane

Beauty springs from it

In the midst of the city or the desert

Within it all things flourish

As it caresses my senses

And nurtures my soul

Sanctuary

~ Gwilda Wiyaka ~

Forward

As beauty is ground to dust under the millstone of expediency and serenity shattered by progress, we find ourselves increasingly isolated from the splendor of the natural world from which we sprang.

As humans left the sanctuary inherent in nature; art, music, and poetry became our links between spirit and the mundane. Now even those are being eradicated from our environment as the arts are eliminated from our schools and workplaces. Beauty is seen as on indulgence to be replaced by the practical cubicle and art is so devalued our artists starve while iron and concrete grow like malignant tumors.

Rather than being lovingly grown, respectfully harvested, artfully cooked and received in gratitude, our food is traumatized in stockyards and butcher plants, genetically modified, microwaved, thrown on Styrofoam, and wolfed down as an afterthought as we drive on iron and concrete to our next appointment.

Yet, whether it is encountered in a forest, cathedral, kiva, or garden, most of us can appreciate the power and beauty of sacred space. While sacred space is the norm in the natural world, it has become a rare commodity in our modern day environment.

In years past, many cathedrals were built on Druid sacred sites aligning the structures with the flow of spirit from nature through the use of sacred geometry. Feng Shui was used to facilitate the natural flow of spirit into structures. These practices and many others took into account the power of the flow of nature we have since come to ignore to our extreme detriment.

The deeper mysteries of any religious practice incorporate principles designed to recreate sacred space in which to worship. From holy water and stone statuary to the steam in a sweat lodge, the four elements of Water, Air, Earth, and Fire are used to set space and raise frequency. Prayers of gratitude, hymns, and chants engage the intent of worshipers adding to the uplifting environment.

Sacred space need not be confined to religious practices. Every activity of our lives can be enhanced and supported by tending to the sanctuary of our environments.

In this workbook we will delve into various methods from multiple cultures used to create this high frequency environment. You will learn to draw on these principals to design a personal practice best suited to your unique needs, lifestyle, and preferences.

Chapter 1:
What is Sacred Space?

Dance, martial arts, gymnastics and almost every other form of movement have one thing in common. Between every maneuver there is a vital and necessary return to center. Without this return to center, balance is lost and the routine disintegrates. In the neutrality of the present moment all future movement is available. By coming from center all of our resources are available to be directed to any given goal. The art of creating sacred space is one of returning to center. The more we renew ourselves through this return, the less our lives disintegrate.

One of the first steps in introducing spirituality into your life and work is creating a space that supports this return to center. Sacred space is created through reestablishing balance, unity, and wholeness. The balance between masculine and feminine, between heaven and earth, the seasons, directions, the elements, between heart and mind can all be brought into play to achieve this end.

If you are working as a healing practitioner, you are probably already familiar with the concept of setting up your space. Massage therapists aim to have a quiet, softly lit setting with meditative music gently playing in the background. A psychotherapist would create an atmosphere that would welcome talking safely and intimately. A medical doctor would endeavor to create a professional setting indicating his/her success and education in order to inspire confidence in the physician's competency.

Each of these settings not only enhances the services offered but also conveys a certain message to the ones seeking the services. How we set up our work settings is partly about how we introduce our clients to what we do.

When decorating our homes we tend to gravitate toward color and design that we find serene and pleasing. While some choose to decorate to impress, most people create a space they feel supported in, surrounding themselves with objects that have meaning to them or have sentimental value.

However, there is much more that we can accomplish by setting space according to a set of spiritual principles that will enhance our professional identities or personal preferences. This workbook will present these principles, and the means of discerning, at any given time, in any given place, how to best create the space you need in the moment.

While the concepts and principles offered within can be employed by the lay person, basic shamanic journey skills greatly enhance the effectiveness of the work. For instruction on the shamanic journey see:

<u>In Touch With Spirit</u>
<u>The Shamanic Journey: Workbook 1</u>

Available at: www.FindYourPathHome.com/store.html, www.Amazon.com or where ever fine books are sold.

Chapter 2:
The Medicine Wheel

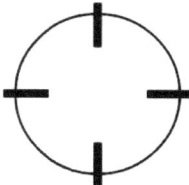

There are at least as many ways of setting up sacred space as there are cultures on the planet, and indeed you might want to draw from many of these. Certain themes run through all cultures, and one of these is the use of the circle, spiral, and the wheel.

A circle is essentially a form with no beginning or end, and has been used as a symbol of protection and wholeness, especially by the ancient Celts. The act of casting a circle is simply that of returning to center. The circle has been used as a sacred symbol purportedly by every indigenous culture on the planet. It is an ancient and powerful symbol that is at the same time, simple yet complex.

The spiral is the evolving expansion of a circle, and is found throughout nature from the shells of mollusks to the cochlea of our inner ears. It is the symbolic expression of growth, especially in which the old form is contained within the new. Cultures as widely separated as the ancient Anasazi and Australian Aboriginals have used the symbol of the spiral. The spiral reminds us that center is not static but ever evolving.

The wheel, a derivative of the circle, was associated with both Saint Catherine and Ezekiel in the Bible. The Hindus and Buddhists adopted the wheel to symbolize the cycles of manifestation, birth, death, and rebirth. Many ancient tribes used the wheel to depict the movements of nature and life, and celebrated the turning points of seasons or milestones. The Mayan Calendar is often depicted as wheels within wheels.

The motion of the spiral is one way to move around a circle or wheel, which is forever evolving rather than just repeating cycles, and is an excellent metaphor for growth and evolution.

One form of the medicine wheel is a circle of rocks built by Native Americans as well as the ancient Celts and Druids according to very exacting and specific principles. It was believed to create a safe and sacred place within its confines in which to access power or information from higher sources. The building of this circle entailed an elaborate ritual that has been passed down through many generations and cultures, thus imbuing it with great power.

The medicine wheel has been used to symbolize and honor the cycles within ourselves and nature. For instance, it can convey the stages of our lives. It also encompasses the four directions (east, south, west, north), the four elements of nature (water, air, earth, fire), and even the four races of humanity (red, yellow, black, white). The circle conveys the wholeness that evolves from the inclusion of each of the four constituents. The spiral motion is also contained within and reminds us that each evolves to the next in a unified seamless manner.

The true power of the medicine wheel lies in its honoring of wholeness. When we honor all that we are, in all our cycles or roles in life, then we can really come into our power. The medicine wheel is one tool we can use to guide us when we set up our sacred space. As I give examples of what can be represented by each of the four directions, please realize that this varies from one culture to another, and is not set in stone. What is more important is what carries meaning for you personally in any given situation.

Chapter 3:
The Four Directions

(A Multi-Cultural View)

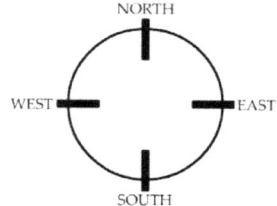

Every indigenous people had tradition and meaning for each of the four directions. Some traditions have more than four directions that they honor, for example, some Lakota have seven: East, South, West, North, Earth, Sky, and Heart. Some Tibetan traditions honor Five: East, South, West, North, and Center, as did some Celtic.

While each tradition has variation in the colors, elements, and animals they attribute to each direction, their basic principles are remarkably similar across the planet.

What I tend to do in my practice is "journey" to find what combination will best serve the people I am doing ceremony for. By drawing from the principles common to all ancient traditions, one can build living ceremony for our modern times.

What follows is a general break down but please bear in mind that there is a great variance even within cultures.

Native American:

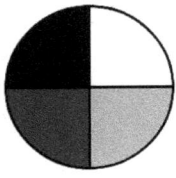

Medicine Wheel

There is so much variance here I hesitate to lump it all together. Following is a generalized example:

East:
Color: Yellow
Season: Spring
Spring Equinox
Sun: Dawn
Age: Birth, Child
Element: Earth
Qualities: Innocence, Learning, Clarity, Illumination
Animal: Eagle

South:
Color: Red
Season: Summer
Summer Solstice
Sun: Mid-day (ever-light)
Age: Mid-life Parents
Element: Fire
Qualities: Passion, Building, Procreation
Animal: Wolf

West:
Color: Black
Season: Fall
Fall Equinox
Sun: Set
Age: Later-life, Grandparents
Element: Water
Qualities: Contemplation, Goals, Introspection, Process
Animal: Bear

North:
Color: White
Season: Winter
Winter Solstice
Sun: Darkness (never-light)
Age: Elders, Great Grandparents, Wise Ones
Element: Air
Qualities: Wisdom, Gratitude, Linking of Ancestral Knowledge
Animal: Buffalo (White)

Celtic:

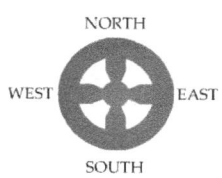
Sacred Circle

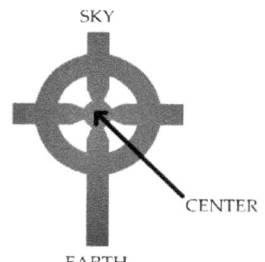
Celtic Cross

East:
Season: Imbolc & Ostara
Dates: February 1 – April 30
Spring Equinox
Sun: Rise
Age: Birth
Element: Earth
Qualities: Beginnings, Birth, Innocence, Justice

South:
Season: Beltane & Litha
Dates: May 1 – July 31
Summer Solstice
Sun: Mid-day
Age: Young Adult
Element: Fire
Qualities: Confidence, Growth, Ambition, Passion, Ardor

West:
Season: Lughnasadh & Mabon
Dates: August 1 – October 31
Fall Equinox
Sun: Set
Age: Middle Age
Element: Water
Qualities: Maturity, Steadiness, Physical Harvest, Nobility

North:
Season: Samhain & Yule
Dates: November 1 – January 31
Winter Solstice
Sun: Dark
Age: Elders
Element: Air
Qualities: Restoration, Renewal, Reflection, Wisdom, Freedom of Spirit, Peace

Tibetan:

Seed of the Universe

Positive Spiritual Energy

Potential Energy

Some Tibetan traditions tend to deal more in duality with the directions representing the extreme imbalance of the characteristics of each. The goal of the enlightened person is to come into center and balance of the same.

East:

The land of the "Have-Nots", in its extreme this is where we live in poverty and lack. We hate those who have and wish to take it from them.

South:

The Tibetan Land of the Dead, this is total victimhood powerlessness and lack of movement. Our lives are at a standstill because we have given over our power with our projection of blame onto others.

West:

The land of the "Haves", in its extreme, this is where we have much and are totally obsessed with obtaining more at any cost to ourselves and others. We live in constant fear that the "Have-Nots" will steal it from us.

North:

Here resides the Goddess of Compassion where we have compassion for ourselves and others. Compassion can have a hard edge, however, and quietly watch us suffer in a detached manner knowing that sometimes more suffering is needed.

These directions are visited by those who wish to be initiated as shaman in order to collect the parts or attributes of one's self that have been lost in that direction. It is believed that only in doing so may a person reach the state of enlightenment and balance required to be a spiritual leader of the people.

This initiation is long, grueling, and intense (I am here to tell you).

Again, this has been an overview and not representative of any one tradition. It is my intent to provide the principles, not appropriate the sacred ceremonies of any one tribe or nation.

Chapter 4
Gratitude

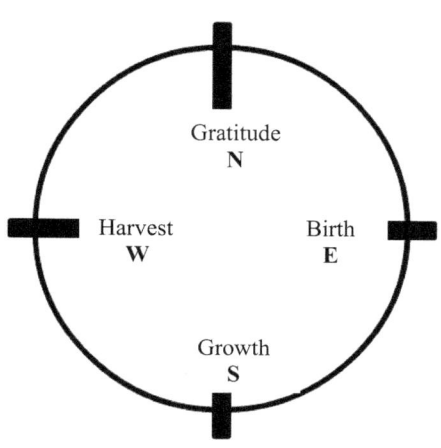

There are four major points on the medicine wheel representing the four cardinal directions. Each of these directions, as discussed earlier, represent different expressions or energies Most medicine wheels are viewed as starting in the east. For this example, we will entertain the direction of East as the birthing of the idea. For instance, we may decide we want a DVD player. The next step is to decide how we will manifest what we've decided we want, which moves us around to the south position or place of action on the wheel. We may take the action to apply for a credit card and purchase the DVD player. In the west position, we harvest and take the DVD into our home and add it to our collection of belongings. In our culture, the position we often forget is the north, the place of gratitude, and instead swing right back to the east and think about what else we want.

Individuals brought up in consumer based societies are trained to disregard the importance of gratitude in order to keep them in a state of perceived lack thus always seeking more to fulfill them. As a result, they are never really sustained, nurtured, or feel they have anything because they are unable to acknowledge what they have by giving gratitude. The satisfaction of a thing is in the honoring of it.

It is very important to be thankful of the spiritual help you receive by expressing gratitude in any way that fits your practice and beliefs. For instance, some may light candles and give prayers of thanks, while others may make an offering of tobacco or cornmeal. Offering gratitude for all the abundance and beauty that spirit brings to you every moment of every day helps you begin to recognize all the gifts, utilize them, and be nurtured by them.

Chapter 5:
Drawing on Ancient Principles

Methods for setting up sacred space are contained in the practices of many cultures. We can adopt or adapt these practices as long as we understand and honor the principles behind the practices. There is an unmistakable power inherent in using existing practices as anything that is repeated by many peoples over many generations seems to gather a power that exceeds that which we can generate on our own as individuals. This is probably due to the fact that mental and emotional elements of rituals have created an energy signature that is stored in the akashic records also called "4-D". The akashic records are a term used to describe all knowledge of human existence stored in the ethers or akasha. These records can be tapped into at any time through use of the shamanic journey.

We already know from modern physics that our consciousness impacts the matter and energy around us. Heisenberg formulated his famous Uncertainty Principle in 1927, which essentially states that the one who observes matter necessarily alters how it behaves merely through the act of observation. In essence, what this is saying is that mind and spirit or energy cannot be separated.

More recently, Roger Nelson, researcher at Princeton's Mechanical and Aerospace Engineering Department, recorded unexpected changes on 40 computers around the world in direct correlation to the attack on the World Trade Center on September 11th, 2011. Similar changes were measured when Princess Diana and Mother Theresa died, as well as during coordinated worldwide meditation projects. Nelson proposes that there is some kind of energy interaction occurring.

Drawing on this knowledge, we see the wisdom in borrowing practices from our ancestors. What follows is an example of how to set up sacred space by using a composite of practices from shamanic, earth-based traditions. This method incorporates the underlying principles that have been consistent across cultures for centuries.

Using this as a foundation, you can begin to develop your own practices, which will hold meaning in your belief system and deepen your personal relationship to Spirit.

The ancients used the medicine wheel as a representation of the powers and principles that were common to all of life. Stepping into the circle was essentially tapping into the energy that emanated from the totality of the life force, of which we are also a part. When we create sacred space, we reenter the place where we are aligned with all that is.

One of the principles drawn upon by the ancients was the belief of the power of Spirit existing in all things and beings. So often we assume the Sacred comes to us in some glorious form, be it a deity or power animal. Yet it is also the air we breathe, the water we drink, the fire that warms us and keeps us alive, and the earth we stand upon. If we can come back into alignment with all of that, we can wield a power commonly thought unavailable to us.

Because the ancients understood that everything is connected, they believed that if you go deep enough, the spirit of the land becomes the spirit of the mother, the earth, and all are contained within your core. You never really have to go anywhere in order to tap into the sacred.

The land and the earth are within you as well as without. So any place that you have ever been, and even places you've never visited but have an affinity with can be accessed through the center of your being. It is all there in our tribal memory, in your DNA, and you can draw on any of these places at any time to create anything you desire.

Chapter 6:
Why We Need Sacred Space

Setting up sacred space and calling in your power before beginning your work is really about aligning with your own power and is an important first step in any shamanic procedure.

In this ancient ceremonial practice you create a link between spirit and the mundane by giving prayers of gratitude, calling in the directions, your power animals and helping spirits. It is important to note that the concept of "calling in" the spirits to create sacred space is a bit deceptive. Spirit is always present. What we are really doing is using the ritual of connecting to the cardinal directions, and our power animals and helping spirits to bring our focus and awareness to the place where we are one with all things.

For those who are sensitive, intuitive, or empathic (which, by the way, is most of us) creating a sacred space within which to live and work is paramount. Many gifted individuals find it necessary to shut down their gifts to limit exposure or bombardment from unwanted interference. This is not necessary if one is trained in how to create sacred space.

Creating sacred space has a more profound influence than one might think. While creating sanctuary can help individuals find home base, fielding unwanted influences and secure peace, it

> There is a Hopi prophecy that roughly states: "When the eagle of the north and the condor of the south fly together there will be peace". There are many ways this has been interpreted, the one we will entertain here is the concept that we need to look at situations and find solutions by both thinking and feeling. Heart and mind must be balanced in order to achieve and maintain male female balance. Thinking and compassion need to be used in equal measure to prevent polarization. When we view issues through both thought and intuition we are getting a binocular view which affords much greater depth perception or more extensive awareness. This translates as greater intelligence providing many more possible solutions to any situation. In turn, we have greater mobility which translates as higher or more expansive frequency.

also returns holiness and high frequency to the entire planet one place at a time.

Sacred, unified space, by its nature, is very expansive. This expansiveness enhances creativity, inspiration, and understanding. It broadens our horizons and by unifying heart and mind it actually more than doubles our intelligence.

By working and living in sacred space everything we do is not only enhanced but the stress of doing it is greatly reduced. Sacred space allows us to work within rather than against the laws of nature. In this way we are supported in what we do while the things that would distract from our project or life are effectively held at bay. In illustration, if we live in a culture that believes the earth is flat, the commonly held belief system would inhibit any thoughts that the earth is other than flat. If we cloister ourselves from the commonly held beliefs, we can then entertain a reality that is different and more expanded. We can do this by intentionally setting sacred space.

Chapter 7:
Tools for Setting Sacred Space

The purpose of setting up sacred space is to:

1) Create a safe and centering place within which to work
2) Call in the power of the spiritual realm to assist in the work

Healing power is optimal when the energy field of the healing location and the healer are both cleansed and brought back into balance with all that is. The process of cleansing is carried out by using personal intent combined with any one of the four elements (Water, Air, Earth, and Fire) as well as plant and mineral helpers.

For instance, merely lighting a candle with the intention of bringing the light into the room can clear out any present imbalanced energies. In some Christian faiths, holy water is sprinkled around the room and on a person who is being blessed. This is also a form of cleansing. Many healers place crystals in the healing room programmed to restore balance. Most common is the use of sacred herbs or incense, which can be burned with the intention of having the rising smoke take away any incompatible frequencies present around the person or the room.

Some of the sacred herbs used by Native American tribes include sage, tobacco, sweet grass, and cedar. The Catholic Church has used frankincense and myrrh. Sandalwood is often used in India. Modern healers will sometimes use essential oils to achieve the same purpose. Each of these plants has cleansing properties. What is important is your clear intent, and that your intention is focused by the ritual you use. If you've ever attended a Catholic Mass, you will recall how everything is performed with deliberate adherence to a ceremony that has been implemented for generations. Through repetition and the agreement of the participants, ceremonies become imbued with power.

Ultimately, it is really up to you which herb to use and when, because these all can accomplish the same function of focusing your intention. However, we also know that certain herbs have been used for centuries to facilitate the clearing of incompatible energies, due to each plants particular frequency. The best course of action is to actually journey to the spirit of the herbs, and they will tell you what they can do for you. That is accessing and using spirit in the now rather than having to learn and memorize and trust old teachings of the uses of various herbs. In other words, it is completely possible that one herb can fill one role that another herb then fills the next day. Be in the moment and use your journey skills or intuition to ask the plant helpers.

This is, after all, the same method ancient medicine people used to develop the herbology practices still used today.

Developing a solid working relationship with your plant, mineral, and element helpers is the key to using them. Once you are familiar and aligned with your helpers, you can access their frequency and bring it into your work or space, even in the absence of the plant, mineral or element. For instance, if you don't have the essential oil you need on hand, yet are well aligned with it, you can bring through your hands the frequency of the essential oil or herb you need. In fact, you can just draw in the frequency of the oil that is needed, without knowing which one it is. You actually change your energy field and frequency to be more like the essence needed to assist the person in their healing. This is a form of shape shifting that requires a long-term working relationship with the frequency of your helpers as well as personal frequency mobility obtained through shamanic healing combined with the mastery of shamanic skills.

Start with the tools you are drawn to or familiar with, and develop a ritual that suits you. We need something to align with at first. Eventually, your body will be the only tool you need. All the master has to do is intend the space be clear and it will energetically manifest.

However, also realize that sometimes the tools you use will help align the intention of the person you are working with, and aid in the healing and in the integration of the healing. You can dance and sing and scream in order to help someone shift frequency, or you can intend your energy to do the same with a gesture or sound. However, the dancing and singing and drumming engage the client to join in the work, and shift the frequency themselves with your backing and support. Hence the work becomes more empowering and lasting.

Chapter 8:
Steps for Setting Sacred Space

All shamanic work begins within, therefore we begin by "purifying" ourselves. This is actually the act of achieving a more expansive frequency from which to do our work. There are various methods for accomplishing this including: smudging oneself with a sacred herb, setting aside our judgments and worries, opening ourselves to thought and intuition, using breath and intention to access personal grounding and centering, drumming and rattling. Start with an organized ritual until you have set up that energetic signature or subroutine for yourself. Later, you can merely intend for it to be so. You may also discover how you have already been cleansing yourself without knowing it. Remember, "cleansing" is simply another term for returning to center through the modulating frequencies.

One of the most important things in creating and maintaining sacred space is to mindfully leave all your worries, agendas, and judgments of self or others outside of the space you are creating. This is the act of entering the center of time or the present moment free of past influences. This can be accomplished by removing your shoes before entering and smudging at the door of a room where space has been set. In a setting where this is not appropriate you can pause by the door and ask silently that a power animal set aside all that will not serve you or the space.

You are always welcome to pick it up again on your way out but I find I am so grateful to not be burdened with my worries and judgments that I am compelled to maintain the peace I encounter in sacred space after I reenter the world.

After you are balanced and centered, cleanse and purify your work or living space using the same techniques.

Next, check in with the land you are on. This is done by taking a middle world journey to the spirit of the land. Identify yourself, tell the land what your intent is and respectfully ask for its permission and cooperation. For instance, if it is an office you are setting up or home you wish to bring into balance, journey to

---

Judge Not

When we judge
Another
We condemn ourselves
To the same
Judgment

Judgment freezes
Us in place
We stagnate
Our spirits die

Furthermore,
We are caught
In a trap
Of our own making

In casting judgment
Upon another
We have become
Victims

As we have projected
Our power to change
Upon the actions
Of another
Which we cannot
Hope to control

There truly is
No judgment
Other than
Self-judgment

"Judge not
Least ye be judged"
Makes perfect sense

It is simply
THE WAY
Of things

~ Gwilda Wiyaka ~

the land that the building is located on. When you cooperate with the spirit of the place, you create unity.

Work counter clockwise, starting in the east, and use the sacred herbs or other tools to clear the space, leaving a door opened or window cracked can be useful to freshen and rebalance the air. Be careful to clear out all the nooks and crannies in the room. You can visually soften your eyes, or use some other technique for tuning in your intuition, and go to the places in the room that seem to draw you. Have the intention of correcting all the frequencies that are incompatible to the purpose that you are intending for the space by attuning the frequencies to become compatible to the intention.

Cleansing of yourself and the space may be done both before and after sessions with a client or before and after setting space in your home. In addition, you may also want to use some ritual for cleansing your clients or guests and family members with their permission. Remember that you have a wide range of tools for doing that, including using your intention, so you can easily accomplish this without offending the beliefs or practices of others. Also realize that when a person enters a space that you have cleansed, he or she will receive some cleansing, too. You can set up a semi-permeable field just outside the door that invites unhelpful frequencies to wait outside. To do this, simply build the field in your imagination then ask your power animal to manifest and maintain it in your space. Your guests are welcome to pick the frequencies or energies back up when they leave if they feel the need to return to their old frequency but the incompatible frequencies will not be present inside to interfere with the purpose of the setting.

When we have set up sacred space, different people will respond differently depending on their true agenda. I have found that people who are sincere about their healing and willing to face their shadow in order to do so will love the environment. Often I see clients come very early for their appointment, or house guests linger, just to spend time in the space. There are others, however, who are unwilling or unable to face their shadow or undergo true change at this time. These folks tend to squirm about, fidget, and seem increasingly uncomfortable. Often these people don't come back more than once if at all. This is Spirit attracting and repelling according to true intent. I have learned not to take it personally or judge the person. I trust all is in order and I will have space for someone I can help or have meaningful exchanges with rather than wasting time on those I cannot.

Sacred space is a living, breathing, moving thing that we need to attend to so that it will bring both ourselves and our clients into balance. It is from this place of balance that we can recognize the imbalances in our lives that are creating our illness and dysfunction. It is for that reason that it needs to be set frequently and deliberately rather than handled like painting a room once and calling it done.

Chapter 9:
Building an Altar

An almost universal tool used to focus intent in setting sacred space is the altar. Building an altar is one way to begin developing personal subroutines to set and hold sacred space. As you walk through the following steps, your mind will learn the principles. However, remember that it is your heart that senses the best way to do this in each setting. After a while, with practice, you will develop a "knowing" as to how to set up sacred space in the moment. The tools used are just that, tools. The master can set space with or without them. Like most rituals, when working with and for others the tools become a common frame of reference used to focus combined intent.

The tools needed for a basic altar are:

1) altar cloth
2) candleholder
3) candle
4) Objects to represent the four directions (stones or small statuary work well)
5) earthen bowl
6) water
7) sage
8) shell or bowl to burn sage in
9) matches or a lighter
10) rattle to call in the directions
11) compass to establish magnetic north

Start by putting your sage in the shell, lighting it then blowing out the flame and use the smoke to cleanse the space you're in, as explained above. This is to shift frequencies that aren't going to serve your purpose. There are no "bad" or negative things, only those things that just don't belong in the space at the time for what you are doing. The intent is not to drive out "evil", but rather to attune frequencies. If you intend to drive out the evil, what you are really doing is polarizing yourself and the environment, thus defeating your purpose.

Cleanse each of your tools in turn before you set them in place. Each act is performed with reverence, gratitude, and quiet deliberation. Sacred space and ceremony are all about being in the moment. Stay totally involved with the task at hand rather than thinking about even the next step of your ritual.

After running it through the sage smoke, set out an altar cloth to define the space that is to be your altar. The altar cloth is like the great mystery. It is the canvas upon which you will paint the design that you are intending. One builds power in the altar by honoring and bringing in the energies of the four directions.

Use a compass to place the altar cloth on the floor or table you are using in such a way as to identify the four directions.

Male and female are honored by the candle and candleholder respectively.

Run the candle through the smoke and bless it with the energy of father sky. Run the candleholder through the smoke and bless it with the energy of mother earth. Then unite them in the sacred union representing passion and co-creation.

 Establish the center, by setting the candle and holder in the center of the altar cloth and blessing its heart. This is accomplished by simply saying "I bless you heart" as you place it on the alter.

 It is important to represent the four elements on your altar.

 An earthen bowl of water works well for the earth and water elements.

Air is already present and the candle, when lit, holds fire.

When placing the next items on your altar it is customary to start in the east, because that is the place of beginnings, and work clockwise to each of the other directions. We work clockwise to build energy and counter clockwise to remove or diminish it.

Starting in the east and working clockwise, place each of your four stones in each of the four directions blessing each to its direction as you set it on the alter.

What else you include on your altar depends on the purpose of your altar, personal preference, and the instructions you receive from your journey work.

You can choose to set out the sacred herbs and have smudging equipment on the altar, to signify the power of transmutation and cleansing. Animal skins, horns, fangs, or feathers may also be included as well as talismans or totems to honor your power animals. What is important is to select things that have meaning for you and your purpose at the time.

For example, I personally like to set a place for each of the four nations or races of people on my altar to hold unity and love for us all during these times of war and polarization. To do this I place patches of cloth, one for each nation; yellow, red, black and white in the corresponding directions.

Other things you can include on your altar are gifts from others. Gifts consciously given can carry great power. Anything that you have that is precious to you and represents something to you can be used to build your altar.

Handmade articles carry a particular power, more so if the artisan applied the principles of shamanic working when creating them. The true arts are a link between Spirit and the mundane.

Appreciation of beauty and gratitude are one in the same. Appreciation, gratitude, and alignment with beauty brings us to that sacred place inside. This is why we use the things that appeal to us for our altar. Deep appreciation of beauty is alignment with spirit.

You can also place patches of colored cloth on each of the four directions of the altar to imbue the patches with the power of the altar. The patches of cloth can be used to absorb the frequency, and then taken with you to your office or some other setting where they will aid you in holding space without a formal altar. You can put them very discreetly in the corresponding four directions of a room where you are working to instantly create sacred space even in environments where a formal setting of space may not be welcomed or understood. Placing these cloth patches around the room, and then saying a quick prayer carries your intent of having sacred space.

Everything you put on your altar can then be used later more effectively because it aligns with and carries the frequency of the altar. Also, the more you use something, the more powerful or aligned it becomes. After you use the same objects for the same purpose, over time, soon all you have to do is just think about the object and imagine it coming into the space in order to bring that frequency into the work you are doing.

Your altar can be anywhere. It makes sense to put it in the center of the room so you can have the circle around it. But it can be anywhere you like. Ultimately, you are setting it with your intent. Space is what we intend it to be. It can be off in a corner or even in a desk drawer. It can be in the medicine pouch you carry around your neck. What is important is that it is tended to regularly in order to keep it aligned and powerful.

Communal altars carry even more power due to the amplification provided by common intent. When you place things on a communal altar built by a circle of people, these items collect the essence of what the group is creating. When you are in such a circle, your healing work is more powerful, and your journeys have increased clarity because all members of the group are holding this sacred reality. When you place personal objects on a communal altar, they will become attuned to the frequency of the group space and can serve as the routes back to the frequency created by the group, outside of time and space.

Therefore, it is of great value to work with a group of other spiritual based practitioners on occasion and to build up this kind of power that each of you can then later draw on to enhance your own healing work.

Chapter 10:
Calling In Your Power

Calling in our power is really about calling upon the spirits all around us and within us, and asking them to assist, protect, intervene, or in some other way be of service to us. In essence, since spirit is already everywhere, what you are really doing when you call in power is aligning yourself with or calling your awareness to what is already present. Spirit is constantly there, waiting to serve us, if only we ask and yield ourselves to a higher power.

The ways of calling in power are as varied as the cultures on the planet. Ultimately, it is our intention to connect with the spiritual that makes the call, so to speak. However, each tradition seems to have some element of sound that is used to call in power or ask for assistance.

Rhythmic sound is a powerful tool for gathering power, whether it is drumming, rattling, chiming, ringing, singing, whistling, chanting, or beseeching.

Rhythm really is the beginning and the end. When we come into the world, the first thing we hear is the beat of our mother's heart, followed by the beat of our own heart. When we are born, our heartbeat is with us, and it is the last thing we hear before we die. Life begins and ends with rhythm.

To create rhythm in order to call in power you can use any number of things. Among the most traditional is the drum or rattle.

Take time to ground and center yourself. Let go of judgment and be present in the moment. Become aware of gravity as it holds you to the earth. When you feel calm, present, and receptive you may begin.

It is traditional to start in the East because east is where the day begins.
Face the East and open your heart to the East. Imagine stepping out into the sunshine after being cold. Allow the warmth to penetrate deep into your heart. Beat your drum or shake your rattle and say a prayer to that direction, asking for its spirit to come to you. Your intent will help you pull the spirit (or frequency) of the East into your heart, and through your heart into your altar or space. Then face the South, West, North, Mother Earth, and Father Sky respectively and do the same things.

Certain Native American traditions work with seven directions, (East, South, West, North, Earth, Sky, and Center). The Celts used a sacred circle with eight spokes that traced the seasons and celebrations of the year. However, each system has varied from tribe to tribe within these cultures.

You may also call in power animals, spirit guides, allies, ancestors, angels, saints, gods, goddesses, ascended masters, your higher self, or any other spirit you have a connection with. Bring them into the center of your altar or whichever direction on the altar they may represent.

Use the journey exercises at the end of this workbook to develop your personal prayers to call in the directions. You can repeat the journeys any time you wish to create sacred ceremony for a different purpose. In this way, you are creating living ceremony for all the events of your life. (For more information on creating ceremony, reference the Path Home Shamanic Arts School class "The Art of Ceremony" and the corresponding workbook.)
FindYourPathHome.com/ws_main.html#artofceremony

At this point, you have created a powerful vortex of energy, which you can then direct into whatever you are doing, be it creating protection or doing healing work. Calling in your power is also a good way to start each day. It helps you set your intention, and keeps you aligned with spirit on a daily basis.

Chapter 11:
Relating to the Elements

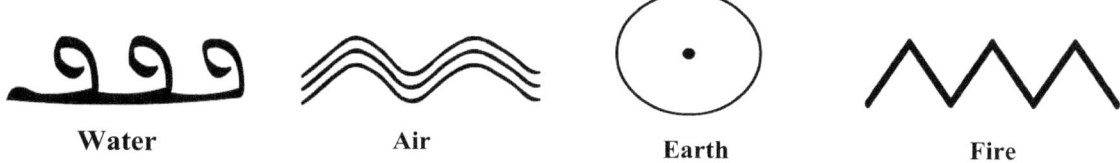

Water   Air   Earth   Fire

The next step in setting your altar and calling in your power it is to align with the energies of the four elements, Water, Air, Earth, and Fire. Each has a place in the four directions and each is alive and well in our bodies. An excellent way to come into Spirit is to bring each of these elements back to balance within ourselves. Our bodies are around 60% water, and our lungs fill and empty with air at the rate of twelve breaths per minute. Our bones are comprised of the minerals of the earth, and fire is present in the mitochondria or power centers in our cells. When we bring the four elements within our bodies into balance, it becomes much easier to enter the state in which we can commune with spirit or interact with all that is.

In order to align with each element in its turn, call upon it while beating your drum or shaking your rattle and "see/imagine" it enter your body. Water may appear as a waterfall washing over you. Air may be a great wind or a summer's breeze. Earth may be a roll in the mud or smelling a handful of rich dirt. Fire may be basking in the sun or burning up in an inferno.

There is also a power animal to represent each element. It may vary but in general, you will have fish for water, birds for air, four leggeds for earth, and reptiles for fire. Perform the journey assignments at the end of the workbook to find which ones will represent the elements for you. After discerning which power animal represents which element you can then envision each one as you call in the elements.

Chapter 12:
Demystifying the Mysterious

I have used traditional concepts and language in talking about the model of creating sacred space including cleansing, accessing spirit, and calling in the directions and elements by use of percussion. At one level of understanding, there is a certain amount of blind faith required to wield spiritual principles on the physical plane. For instance, unless we look deeper into the energetic principles these rituals employ, one can feel rather awkward standing shaking a rattle at the east and calling out to an invisible, a "spirit". This can leave beginning students with the impression that they have to adhere to a particular belief system or religion in order to practice shamanism. This is far from the truth.

As above so below, the same principals of physics that apply on the physical level also apply on the energetic. The techniques shared here are simply rituals designed to focus intent in order to effect a change in the energetic plane. If you decide to study further and take advanced Map Home or Path Home shamanic classes we delve deeply into energetic patterns and frequencies that affect each of us and the planet. We also look at the spiritual evolution available to us at this time.

For now, let's agree that we have evolved over the last two hundred plus years and have the capacity to view these energetic concepts from a more practical and functional approach rather than a mystic one requiring blind faith. Backed by scientific principles not available to our ancestors we can understand the inner workings or principles behind "spirit" or frequency. This deeper understanding gives us much more flexibility in developing our personal practice.

Our ancestors were unaware that radio waves or radiation passes through solid matter. To have tried to explain it to them would have resulted in disbelief. The common belief system based upon the knowledge base of the times would not support this concept. It was much more believable that the medicine man would "scare out the evil spirits" which were causing illness.

Everything expresses according to frequency. As frequency shifts, so does expression. At cold temperatures, water molecules move more slowly at a lower frequency and express as a solid in the form of ice. When the temperature rises the molecules move more quickly and the water becomes less dense. It becomes liquid. More heat and greater frequency produces steam and so on. Rudimentary my dear Watson.

The higher the frequency the less force required to cause change. For instance, we can use our breath to move steam. By blowing on it we can cause steam to shift position while trying to move a block of ice with the same method will result in nothing more than hyperventilation. In order to move the ice you would have to use something equally as dense such as your hand while applying more force.

Our intent expresses through very high level frequency. Once things are already present in physical form they become dense and require equally dense intervention to change them. It follows that we can achieve change through intent only in the higher frequencies where our intent can have an effect. Through conscious and focused use of intent we modulate frequency thereby setting up the optimum energetic environment for matter to form around rather than trying to move matter once already formed. We modulate frequencies in order to provide the environment required for our purpose.

Setting sacred space is the act of using ritual to focus our intent in order to set frequencies and facilitate energy flow to support our purpose. In other words, we combine purpose and intent in order to modulate frequency. This is much like tuning a radio in order to change stations, accessing a musical genre more appropriate to the task at hand.

When we set sacred space we first must be clear on purpose. If my purpose is to support sleep in a bedroom, different frequencies would be used than if I were enlivening an exercise facility. Through the use of the principles outlined above, it is not only possible to set the frequency of one's home but each individual room as well. The more specific we become, the more we are supported by our personal space.

Once we have decided upon purpose, we need to set intent. That is the simple act of deciding to "do it". At the higher, less dense frequencies the act of deciding carries power and affects a change, much like blowing on steam.

We then modulate the frequency by holding purpose in our vision and intent in our will. This initiates a complicated interaction that takes place in our chakra system. Fortunately, we don't have to understand it at this point any more than we need to understand the inner workings of the radio in order to change stations so we won't go into it here. Like the radio, the rituals listed above help focus and amplify this process. By having an altar or articles present in an environment that represent our purpose and intent we are constantly reminded to maintain the frequencies that support our objective.

Chapter 13:

Stuff

No discussion about sacred space is complete without discussing the stuff we put in it. Everything we own has frequency. This frequency is actually a conglomeration of frequencies from the composition of the thing itself, to every hand that touched it in its creation and thereafter. It also carries the wishes, hope, and dreams we may have held for it when we acquired it. If it was a gift, it carries another whole agenda from the giver.

All of these energies, wishes, hopes, and agendas are probably mostly unconscious. For instance, how many of us are conscious and purposeful all day at work? Do we do what we are doing or does our mind wander to what is going on in the rest of our life. Are we working with gratitude and blessing toward whoever will end up with what we are making or doing or do we resent spending our time on it?

When we purchase something do we do it in gratitude to all that went into creating it from the sand melted into glass to the fire providing the heat? Or do we unconsciously hope the smashing red color will make our house look more impressive to others? Do we hang our happiness on the acquisition destining it to failure? When we give someone a gift do we truly release it to them or are there strings all over it? Do you have the implied wish of *"Now you will be grateful"; "Next time I want something you will remember this expensive gift I gave you;"* or *"Now you will love me"*?

Every one of these conscious or unconscious intents imbues the article establishing its frequency and when you have it in your environment, it influences the overall frequency in your home or office, on your body or wherever it is placed.

As we contemplate the above, it is hard not to look around at what surrounds us and throw our hands up in despair. I won't lie to you; it is a big job, this living consciously. Content yourself with the thought that anything you do helps. It is not a matter of perfection. Holding that in mind, I will share some guidelines for acquisition, possession, and release that have helped me.

1) **Spring cleaning**: I go through my home or office on a regular basis and reset the energy one room at a time. First I decide the purpose of that particular room. Then I evaluate everything in it to see if it is aligned with that purpose. (Things of beauty have purpose as beauty by its very nature is high frequency.) I remove the things that are not serving the environment and set them aside for further evaluation. I physically clean the room from top to bottom and clear every object in it.

2) **Blessing things to their purpose:** Every article I have decided belongs in the room I journey to, giving gratitude for its original constituents and all the hands that went into it reaching me. This simple act sends high frequency down the line of its creation not only raising its frequency but offering gratitude to those that made it. After deciding the purpose an article will serve, I bless it to that purpose. If the article will represent abundance, I hold it and state, "you will hold the frequency of abundance" before placing it in the north-west corner of the room. If the article is my bed, I say "I bless you to support my sleep" and so on.

3) **Purposeful placement:** Using the very basic principles of Feng Shui or simply the four directions, I place the furniture and articles in the room to create flow and beauty. This also serves to make a living altar out of each room.

4) **Reducing drag:** Everything we own actually owns a piece of our energy. If we own things that remind us of someone else, that person becomes an influence in our environment and therefore our personal frequency. By removing the things that hold us to a frequency that may not be in agreement with who we now are or hope to become, we support our purpose. This in effect, reduces the energetic "drag" that we must push through to achieve what we have chosen in any circumstance.

5) **Discernment:** By now I have created a pile of "doesn't serve" articles. I go through this pile and discern if it belongs anywhere in my environment. If it doesn't, I journey to pull my energy out of it and release it to its next purpose, where ever and with whom ever that may be. When we just throw or give things away out of hand, guess what? ……we throw or give away part of our energy. The good news is in shamanism we are not bound by time or space. We can always journey back to just before we got rid of something and release it properly.

I understand what a seemingly herculean undertaking this is. My advice, pick a single room that is very important to you to start with and focus on it. When you have gone through the procedure once, it is so rewarding that you may find yourself encouraged to continue.

My children often tease me about my "Zen" environment. I simply respond, "Consider the alternatives".

Chapter 14:
Sacred Space a State of Grace

Purpose and intent are only effective in the present moment. Any daily practice, such as meditation, drumming, singing, dancing, or invoking the four directions, helps you come back into the present moment. By focusing on the balance between the cardinal directions and elements we regain our personal balance of center. The center of each of us is the connecting point to all that is, and is the only place from which we can access power. Yet we often look outside of ourselves for answers and fulfillment.

Our ability to access and maintain center in the present moment is limited by our past damage. Anywhere we have been damaged we have developed defenses and compensations that take us out of our natural expression. This compromises our ability to come into balance with the present moment. Damage comes in many forms; simple socialization being one. From childhood, we are taught we are not acceptable like we are. We are lead to believe that we must change or act in particular ways in order to be loved. This blocks us from accessing the core of what we are.

In order to truly master shamanic skills it is necessary to obtain shamanic healing of the damage we have sustained. One such healing technique is known as soul retrieval. This shamanic procedure helps us reconnect with our natural expression and reestablish the sanctity of our personal beings. For more information on soul retrieval or to find a certified shamanic practitioner visit: www.FindYourPathHome.com/practitioners.html

Sacred space really starts with us. That is where it begins, and that is where it ends. The main ingredient in setting up sacred space is *becoming* sacred space. It is the position you come from that imbues your space with sacredness. Fortunately, we

---

Grace

There is a place
Deep in the core
Of each of us

Where peace resides

Journey inward
Past your beliefs
Past your separation
Past your pain

To where the elements
Dance

As they draw up from the
Earth
Down from the
Sky

To form the very
Essence
Of which
We are made

Here we are all
The same
Here we are all
One

This is Grace

~ Gwilda Wiyaka ~

do not have to be totally healed and processed to achieve this. Through the techniques shared here we can set aside our damage and come from the neutrality of our heart.

At the same time, you cannot live constantly in a state of non-polarization in a polarized reality such as the one we all presently inhabit. You wouldn't be able to interface with others, and would be of no service to anyone. It is very important to be gentle with yourself in this process, because it is not a matter of staying in center; it is a matter of returning to center. Centering is not a static thing.

The first step to creating sacred space is to access it within ourselves. This is achieved through a continuing process of healing and releasing those things that stand in the way of our access to inner peace by always working on ourselves. This process affords us increasing access to our personal power and clarity.

All of us are already very powerful. It is our birthright. What brings us into that power is becoming conscious of when and how we use it. Once we bring our use of power into consciousness, we can then, through discipline and the development of subroutines, use it automatically. The rituals, principles, and objects are simply used to develop subroutines and help set intent. Dogmatic adherence to ritual is for those who can't access spirit any other way. For the rest of us, it is best to access spirit in the moment, and create a ritual that best applies at that time, in that circumstance, and for that particular purpose. This is living ritual, and is the true shamanic way.

When all is said and done, sacred space is finding the center of our beings where the power and grace of the universe, our true nature resides. Through sacred ritual and intent, we can then bring it into our world and lives. This is the pathway to heaven on earth. Every time you take the effort to create and maintain sacred space, you have created a little piece of heaven.

I am grateful you have joined me in the joyous task of creating heaven for us all.

Chapter 15:
Sacred Space Journey Assignments

Finding Your Inner Sanctum

30 minute journey (FindYourPathHome.com/store.html or www.Amazon.com)
(Track 3 on "On Wings of Spirit" or "Betwixt and Between" CD or MP3)

Call in your power animal and tell it you would like to journey to find out how you can create or access sacred space within your own being.

Ask if it will be a lower or upper world journey.

Journey with your power animal to upper or lower world as instructed.

When you arrive, call out that you would like to find out how you can create or access sacred space within your own being.

1. Once the journey has unfolded, ask for a symbol that you can visualize in the future helping take you to your inner sanctum quickly.
2. Ask what you need to heal or clear in order to access your inner sanctum more easily.
3. Ask to be taken to your inner sanctum. Just *be* there until the call back beat sounds.

When you return, journal your experience and write a poem that expresses your experience of your inner sanctum.

Repeat part 3 of this journey frequently. It will help you find calm and peace in a world badly in need of both.

Access this place of inner sanctum before performing any sacred ceremony.

Setting up a Personal Altar Journey Assignments:

Use the following journey exercise to help you access the information you need to set up your altar. Once you create your own process for setting up your personal altar you will repeat the procedure over and over, giving it the power of ritual, which really sets these energies for you. By journeying to get the information, you find out what practices best align with you, your heritage, and strengths.

The Altar

30 minute journey (FindYourPathHome.com/store.html or www.Amazon.com)
(Track 3 on "On Wings of Spirit" or "Betwixt and Between" CD or MP3)

Call in your power animal and tell it you would like to journey to find out how to set up your altar.

Ask if it will be a lower or upper world journey.

Journey with your power animal to upper or lower world as instructed.

Once there, ask your power animal to help you find out how you are to set up an altar. Be sure to include the purpose of the altar. (Personal, for a group or event etc.)

Ask:

1. What is the best location for your altar?
2. What colors to use for each direction?
3. Which elements go in each direction and how to represent each one?
4. What objects you are to include and where?
5. Which animal for each direction?

Journal the information when you return from your journey.

If the information becomes more than you can accurately remember, take more than one journey and journal each time.

Set about locating the articles your journey indicated. You may be surprised how many of them you already have. Also surprising is how they find their way into our lives when we are in the process of gathering them. Journaling where and how our sacred objects come to us can also map our process and bring more insight.

Remember to clear each object then journey and give gratitude for everything involved in bringing the object to you before blessing it to its new purpose.

Calling In Your Power

4 - 15 minute journeys (www.FindYourPathHome.com/store.html or www.Amazon.com)
(Track 4 on "On Wings of Spirit" or "Betwixt and Between" CD or MP3)

Call in your power animal and tell it you would like to journey to each of the four directions. State which direction you would like to visit each time you go. For example, "This time I would like to journey to the east."

This will be a middle world journey so remember, journey with your power animal and don't talk to strangers.

"See" yourself traveling middle world to the direction you ask to be taken.

When you arrive, ask to speak to the spirit of that direction.

When it shows up, (if in doubt, ask your power animal if this is indeed the spirit of the direction you seek) respectfully introduce yourself. Tell it you are learning how to call in power and you would like to know how to call it in.

Ask:

1. What it would like to be called?
2. What power animal it would like to have represent it?
3. What element would it like to hold for you?
4. What particular power or gifts will it bring into your practice?
5. Ask for a song or prayer to call it in (you may want to take a separate journey on this question).

Journal the information when you return from your journey.

If the information becomes more than you can accurately remember, take more than one journey and journal each time.

Journey to see which power animal represents each element

4 - 15 minute journeys (www.FindYourPathHome.com/store.html or www.Amazon.com)
(Track 4 on "On Wings of Spirit" or "Betwixt and Between" CD or MP3)

Call in your power animal and tell it you would like to journey to find a power animal to represent each of the four elements. State which element you would like to visit each time you go. For example, "This time I would like to journey to the element of water."

Ask if it will be a lower or upper world journey.

Journey with your power animal to upper or lower world as instructed.

When you get there, call out for the power animal that will come be with you to represent the element you have chosen to journey on.

Bear in mind it may be one you already have or one that is new to you.

When your animal shows up ask:

1. What it would like to be called?
2. What particular power or gifts will it bring into your practice?
3. How it would like to be cared for and fed?
4. Ask for a song or prayer to call it in.

Journal the information when you return from your journey.

About Path Home Shamanic Arts School

Path Home Shamanic Arts School is a unique Colorado State Certified Occupational School designed to bring into modern times and healing practices the ancient, tried and true shamanism skills of our indigenous peoples. At Path Home, we understand that there is a growing need for well-trained spiritual healers and stewards in our modern communities.

Path Home offers an intensive Shamanic Practitioner Certification Program specifically designed to prepare our students to build their private practice treating spiritual illness. Our graduates are trained to enter the professional world interfacing with mainstream health care practitioners. The Shamanic Practitioner Certification training is a two-year, 386 hour program that produces competent, well prepared shamanic practitioners to treat the spiritual illness of today's people.

The **Path Home Shamanic Instructors Certification Program** trains individuals to teach shamanic skills through the use of shamanic techniques. In order to effectively teach the practice you need to not only be proficient in the form itself, but be able to track your students in non-ordinary reality. Path home teaches its instructors this and many other unique skills creating exceptional teachers.

Map Home is a branch of Path Home that offers classes, workshops and healing retreats for individuals interested in personal growth and development and in learning to live in a shamanic way. During these intense, rapidly changing times through 2012 and well beyond, Path Home prides itself in supporting spiritual evolution by preparing individuals to not only survive but to thrive in the newly emerging landscape.

For more information on Path Home Shamanic Arts School or Map Home Personal Growth Programs, contact us:

www.FindYourPathHome.com
TouchIn@FindYourPathHome.com
303-775-3431

About Path Home's State Certification

Path Home Shamanic Arts School is a Colorado State certified occupational school. This means that Path Home has gone through a rigorous certification program that insures its founder, director and instructors have the qualifications to teach the shamanic arts. In addition, the student's interests are guarded with bonded tuition to certified curriculum and established refund policies. The catalogs and all four certification programs are approved and on file with the state of Colorado-- this insures consistency and quality of the classes.

Why did we go through all the expense, paper work, scrutiny and time to obtain certification from the State of Colorado for Path Home?

- In order to teach anything in the State of Colorado that can be used in an existing job or as a job, certification by the state is legally required.
- Integrity: Integrity was and is our core motivation for creating the School. The Shamanic Arts are a viable powerful healing modality that requires extensive training as well as personal growth and development to wield responsibly. Spiritual healing is, in its own way, as complex as physical healing. For this reason, we feel it is irresponsible in the extreme to perform spiritual healings after having learned a few techniques at workshops.
- While the physical and emotional/mental healing arts are regulated as of yet, the spiritual ones are not. For this reason, Path Home has chosen to hold itself to the exacting standards we feel the field not only warrants but deserves.
- Path Home Shamanic Arts school trains and certifies "Shamanic Practitioners" not "Shaman". We feel that the indigenous shaman from all cultures are in a class all their own and we do not profess to offer in two years what takes life times and generations to achieve.
- Our programs are designed to produce competent well trained Shamanic Practitioners of integrity to take on the spiritual illnesses of our culture today. It is for this reason we feel that our program needs to stand up to the quality and exacting standards of today's educational systems.

Path Home's listing with The Division of Private Occupational Schools (DPOS):
http://highered.colorado.gov/DPOS/Students/directory.asp?residency=in

Resources

CD's and MP3's available for this workbook

On Wings of Spirit (quad drumming for the shamanic journey)
Betwixt and Between: (double drumming for the shamanic journey)

Available at: www.FindYourPathHome.com/store.html or www.Amazon.com

Shamanic Healing

Path Home offers long distance shamanic healing sessions.
To schedule an appointment with a Path Home certified shamanic practitioner contact us:

www.FindYourPathHome.com
TouchIn@FindYourPathHome.com
303-775-3431

Additional books, CD's, and MP3's by Gwilda

Available at: www.FindYourPathHome.com/store.html or www.Amazon.com

Books:

In Touch With Spirit, The Shamanic Journey: Workbook 1

The shamanic journey is the cornerstone of all shamanic divination practices. Mastering this ancient form can effectively connect you to your own spiritual information and guidance. **In Touch With Spirit** was written by Gwilda Wiyaka, CSI, founder and director of Path Home Shamanic Arts School, as a text to accompany the School's Shamanic Journey and Power Animals/ Helping Spirits classes. The easily understood principles and techniques found within are empowering and life changing.

CD's & MP3s:

On Wings of Spirit (quad drumming for the shamanic journey)
Betwixt and Between: (double drumming for the shamanic journey)

One People One Nation (ancient and modern shamanic songs)
Winds of Time by: StarFaihre (ancient and modern shamanic songs)

Notes

Notes

Notes

www.ingramcontent.com/pod-product-compliance
Lightning Source LLC
LaVergne TN
LVHW081400060426
835510LV00016B/1920